Biblical Foundation 7

Learning to Fellowship with God

by Larry Kreider

House To House Publications
Lititz, Pennsylvania USA

Learning to Fellowship with God

Larry Kreider

Updated Edition © 2002, Reprinted 2003, 2005
Copyright © 1993, 1997, 1999
House to House Publications
11 Toll Gate Road, Lititz, PA 17543
Telephone: 800.848.5892
Web site: www.dcfi.org

ISBN 1-886973-06-7
Design and illustrations by Sarah Sauder

CONTENTS

Books in this Series

This is the seventh book in a twelve-book series designed to help believers to build a solid biblical foundation in their lives.

1 **Knowing Jesus Christ as Lord**
   God's purpose for our lives through a personal relationship with Jesus

2 **The New Way of Living**
   True repentance and faith toward God

3 **New Testament Baptisms**
   Four baptisms including baptism in water and baptism in the Holy Spirit

4 **Building For Eternity**
   The hope of the resurrection, the laying on of hands and eternal judgment

5 **Living in the Grace of God**
   Applying God's grace to everyday living

6 **Freedom from the Curse**
   Christ brings freedom to every area of our lives

7 **Learning to Fellowship with God**
   How to deepen our relationship with Jesus Christ

8 **What is the Church?**
   Finding our place in God's family

9 **Authority and Accountability**
   How to respond to leadership and fellow believers God places in our lives

10 **God's Perspective on Finances**
   How God wants His people to handle money

11 **Called to Minister**
   Every Christian's call to serve

12 **The Great Commission**
   Our purpose for living on this planet

A corresponding *Biblical Foundations for Children* book is also available (see page 63).

Biblical Foundations

Introduction

The foundation of the Christian faith is built on Jesus Christ and His Word to us, the Holy Bible. This twelve-book *Biblical Foundation Series* includes elementary principles every Christian needs to help lay strong spiritual foundations in his or her life.

In this seventh Biblical Foundation book, *Learning to Fellowship with God,* we learn God wants to know us personally! We're going to learn how to fellowship with God through meditating on God's Word and praying and worshiping Him. We will discover how to develop a close, intimate relationship with God through Jesus Christ as we learn to hear His voice.

In this book, the foundation truths from the Word of God are presented with modern day parables that help you easily understand the basics of Christianity. Use this book and the other 11 *Biblical Foundation* books to lay a solid spiritual foundation in your life, or if you are already a mature Christian, these books are great tools to assist you in discipling others. May His Word become life to you today.

God bless you!

Larry Kreider

How to Use This Resource

Personal study

Read from start to finish as an individual study program to build a firm Christian foundation and develop spiritual maturity.
- Each chapter has a key verse excellent to commit to memory.
- Additional scriptures in gray boxes are used for further study.
- Each reading includes questions for personal reflection and room to journal at the end of the book.

Daily devotional

Use as a devotional for a daily study of God's Word.
- Each chapter is divided into 7-day sections for weekly use.
- Additional days at the end of the book bring the total number of devotionals to one complete month. The complete set of 12 books gives one year's worth of daily devotionals.
- Additional scriptures are used for further study.
- Each day includes reflection questions and a place to write answers at the end of the book.

Mentoring relationship

Use for a spiritual parenting relationship to study, pray and discuss life applications together.
- A spiritual father or mother can easily take a spiritual son or daughter through these short Bible study lessons and use the reflection questions to provoke dialogue about what is learned.
- Read each day or an entire chapter at a time.

Small group study

Study this important biblical foundation in a small group setting.
- The teacher studies the material in the chapters and teaches, using the user-friendly outline provided at the end of the book.

Taught as a biblical foundation course

These teachings can be taught by a pastor or other Christian leader as a basic biblical foundation course.
- Students read an assigned portion of the material.
- In the class, the leader teaches the assigned material using the chapter outlines at the end of the book.

CHAPTER 1

Knowing God Through His Word

KEY MEMORY VERSE

...The words I have spoken to you
are spirit and they are life.
John 6:63

How can we get to know such an awesome God?

Let's imagine that you are jogging down a street in Washington D.C. and the President of the United States jogs by. You hail him with a greeting, "Hello, Mr. President." Does the president know you? Do you know him? Probably not. You may know all about the president, but it's one thing to know a lot of facts about him; it's a different thing to actually know him personally.

In the same way, many people know all about God, but they don't really know Him in a personal way. God is infinite, the creator of the universe, the original being, the sovereign ruler of all that is. No one created Him (Acts 17:23-25), He has always been around and will continue eternally unchanged (Hebrews 13:8). How can we get to know this infinite God when we are but finite humans? How can our minds even begin to comprehend Him?

There is one God
1 Corinthians 8:4
Ephesians 4:6; James 2:19

We can get to know God through Jesus Christ. God has made Himself known through Jesus. He is made real to us through a relationship with His Son whom He sent to earth to do His will. Jesus came to personally encounter us and die for our sins so we can live forever. *Now this is eternal life: that they may know you, the only true God, and Jesus Christ, whom you have sent (John 17:3).*

According to the Bible, eternal life involves getting to know, commune, and fellowship with our God who is made known through His Son Jesus Christ whom He sent. God wants to know us personally! In this book, we're going to learn how to fellowship with God through meditating on God's Word and praying and worshiping Him. We will discover how to develop a close, intimate relationship with God through Jesus Christ.

Beforehand, however, it is important to understand who God is. We believe in and worship one God. When God spoke to Moses in the ancient days, He revealed Himself as One. Centuries later, when Jesus was asked to choose the greatest commandment, Jesus quoted those same words of long ago...*Hear, O Israel, the Lord our God, the Lord is one...(Mark 12:29).*

REFLECTION
According to John 17:3, how can we get to know God?
Do you know God or only know about Him?

✱ Thru God's word & the word made flesh the man-God Jesus Christ
✱ I Know Him.

The Bible clearly teaches there is only one God. Yet we know from scripture that God is Father, God is Jesus and God is Spirit. That does not mean that God is three. There is only one God whom we love and worship. So how can He be one and yet three?

When three equals one

According to the Bible, God is one God who is three persons. The term *Trinity* is used to describe this concept. When Jesus said we should go into all nations making disciples, the three persons of the Trinity are linked together...*in the name of the Father and of the Son and of the Holy Spirit (Matthew 28:19)*.

The Bible also tells us in the book of Genesis, "Let *Us* make man in Our image" (Genesis 1:26). When the world was created, God the Father, God the Son, and God the Holy Spirit worked together to create the earth and all that is on it. God the Father, God the Son, and God the Holy Spirit always were in existence.

The Father, Son and Holy Spirit are coequal, coeternal members. Although this concept is not easy for us to understand, our God is one essence existing in three distinct persons who share a divine nature—God our Father who is in Heaven, God the Son whom He sent to earth, and God the Holy Spirit who dwells in every believer who has been born again through faith in Jesus Christ.

The Trinity
God is one essence existing in three distinct persons who share a divine nature: Father, Son and Holy Spirit: Matthew 3:16-17; 28:19
2 Corinthians 13:14
Ephesians 4:4-6
1 Peter 1:2; Jude 20-21

The three are not three gods, or three parts or expressions of God, but are three persons so completely united that they form the one true and eternal God.[1] To fathom this, our minds and hearts must be stretched to hold a greater God than we can even imagine! God is so great—our finite minds cannot easily understand. It sometimes helps to look at the things He has created. In nature, we find things that take different forms and have different effects on our senses, yet are still one.

For example, water takes on three different forms. Water is converted into an invisible vapor or gas (steam) by being heated. Ice is the crystalline form of water made solid by cold temperatures. No matter what its form (water, steam or ice), it is still water.

Another example from nature is the sun. According to scientists, no one has actually seen the sun because it is so powerful. When we look at the sun, we do not see the star itself, but we can clearly see the rays of sun that shine on the earth. From the sun itself, through its rays, we have light and heat, and something mysterious makes plants grow (through the process of photosynthesis). We can conclude that the sun is the sun—one entity. Yet, the sun is light; the sun is heat; the sun is growth-life.

All of this is true without contradiction. It is still the sun.

Although these illustrations from what has been created may help us to understand the idea of God being One—Father, Jesus, Spirit—they are not enough. We cannot decide who God is and

Name the three persons of the Trinity. According to Hebrews 11:6, how can we really get to know God?

✝ Father - Son - Spirit
✝ Thru seeking Him.

what He is like based on what our eyes see, our ears hear or our hands touch. We must put our faith in God Himself. We must choose what to believe about Him based on His Word.

We must spend our lives seeking Him and getting to know Him better. We must read the Bible and do what it says. How can we understand Him without knowing and loving Him? How can we see Him without believing and obeying Him? No one person can fully explain God to another. We must each seek Him and know Him. *And without faith it is impossible to please God, because anyone who comes to him must believe that he exists and that he rewards those who earnestly seek him (Hebrews 11:6).*

[1] *Full Life Study Bible*, NIV, Life Publishers International, 1992, p.1479.

Jesus is God

When we earnestly seek God, we find Him through Jesus Christ. Before getting into the remainder of the chapter, let's look briefly at the claims of Jesus. As Christians, we must believe He is who He said He is, because it persuades us of His deity.

Very few people will say that a man called Jesus of Nazareth never existed. There are many ancient writings, both religious and secular, that confirm to His place in history. There are many, however, who will say that He was just a good man or a prophet. Many believe that He was just a man, flesh and blood, like the rest of us. The religious leaders of Jesus thought the same, and they wanted to stone Him. The things Jesus said made them furious (see John 10:24-38) because Jesus boldly claimed that He was God. They accused him of blasphemy because only God has the right to say He is God.

How can we know that Jesus is who He claimed to be? Jesus' answers to the stone-throwers pointed to four reasons we can be certain Jesus is who He said He is:

Scripture: Jesus continually pointed to and affirmed the scripture. He knew the scriptures and obeyed them. He fulfilled all the prophecies of the Messiah.

Sonship: According to prophecies, Jesus was born of a virgin in Bethlehem. Jesus called God "Father" and stressed his unique relationship as His only begotten Son.

Actions: Jesus told His accusers not to believe Him unless He did what His Father does. Jesus' whole life was characterized by a constant awareness of the Father's will. He said and did what the Father said and did. Though many tried to accuse Him, they never were able to because He had done no wrong.

Miracles: If none of that will persuade us to believe, the miracles should. He restored sight to the eyes of a man born blind. He made the deaf hear and speak. He made the lame walk, cured lepers and made many other sick people well. Demons obeyed Him without hesitation, knowing who He was. He had authority over nature, calming a storm with a word. He changed water to wine and multiplied one boy's lunch to feed thousands. He walked on water. He made accurate predictions about what people would do and what events would take place. Greatest of all, Christ rose from the dead. Death could not rule over Him! Jesus' resurrection is the real proof and demonstration of His deity.

REFLECTION

Write down the four reasons confirming that Jesus is who He said He is. Did Jesus ever deny that He is One with God?

It is interesting to see that with all Jesus' claims and with all His power, He never denied that God is One. He simply said that He and the Father are One. Jesus was not merely a man or prophet. Jesus is who He claimed to be. He is God's Son. He is One with the Father. Because of who He is, Jesus was able to reconcile the world to the Father.

Learning to Fellowship with God

God's Word is life to us

God wants us to get to know Him. The scriptures say in Revelation 3:20, *Here I am! I stand at the door and knock. If anyone hears my voice and opens the door, I will come in and eat with him, and he with me.* This is an invitation! When we receive Jesus, we are invited to sit down to a friendly meal together. This is a picture of the intimacy that God wants to have with us.

How can we build a relationship with Him? First of all, we build a relationship with the Lord by meditating on the Word of God. John 6:63 teaches us, *the Spirit gives life; the flesh counts for nothing. The words I have spoken to you are spirit and they are life.* Many Christians today find themselves dried up spiritually because they have not taken God's Word as spirit and life. The Bible is not just a set of good principles and historical facts; it is life to us! As we meditate on His Word, we build a relationship with Him. He speaks to us through His Word.

A friend of mine stepped onto an elevator a few years ago, and to his surprise, there stood Billy Graham the renowned evangelist. He only had a split second to ask Mr. Graham one quick question, "Mr. Graham, if you were a young man like me, what word of advice would you have?"

The evangelist looked at him with the sincerity that has marked his life and said, "Read the Bible and get to know the Word of God." The evangelist had learned, after walking with the Lord for many years, that the best way to know God is to know His Word.

In reality, Jesus and His Word are one. *In the beginning was the Word, and the Word was with God, and the Word was God (John 1:1).* To know Jesus is to know His Word. To love Jesus is to love His Word. You cannot separate the Word of God and Jesus Christ. Revelation 19:13b says...*his name is the Word of God.*

A few years ago, I read the results of a survey that produced some startling findings. It said that one-quarter of Protestant church leaders are not born again Christians and only half of all church leaders (53%) believe that there are moral truths that are absolute.[1] That's one of the reasons why spiritual power has gone from many churches today! If we don't believe that the Bible is the Word of God—that it is actually Jesus speaking to us as His people—we are bankrupt of spiritual power. God will not be able to move supernaturally in our lives. Unbelief will hinder God's supernatural work. Even Jesus could not do many miracles in His hometown because of the unbelief of some of His own family members (John 7:1-5).

[1] Barna Research Online, www.barna.org, "Leadership" statistics and analysis in this archive come from national surveys conducted by Barna Research, 1997.

God's Word renews our minds

Romans 12:2 says, *Do not conform any longer to the pattern of this world, but be transformed by the renewing of your mind....*

What does it mean to not be conformed to the pattern of this world? The *world* mentioned here refers to our present age or world system. This *world* is subject to the devil—the god of this world (2 Corinthians 4:4) and is consequently filled with sin and suffering.

In this age, Satan uses the world's ideas, morality, philosophies, mass media, etc. to oppose God's people and His Word. The world's system is one of selfishness that is under Satan's rule. In contrast, God's kingdom is a kingdom of love.

One translation of this verse in the Bible says we should not be "put into the world's mold." Have you ever taken a box of gelatin, mixed it with hot water, and poured it into a mold? After it has time to chill, the gelatin is shaped like the mold. The Bible says that if we do not separate ourselves from this world's system, we will end up molded like the world.

Renewing our minds is like taking a car with an old engine to a mechanic. After the mechanic puts in new parts, greases and adjusts them correctly, the engine runs like new. If we do not renew our minds by the Word of God by getting "greased and adjusted," we will begin to think and act like the world's system around us. The Word of God actually cleanses our minds from the thoughts and mindsets of the world system around us. It is like taking a spiritual bath on a regular basis. Living in this world causes us to get spiritually dirty. The Word of God cleanses us and renews our minds. Ephesians 5:25-26 tells us, *Christ loved the church and gave himself up for her to make her holy, cleansing her by the washing with water through the word.*

In the book of Acts, we read that Paul, the apostle, was impressed when he met a group of people called the Bereans (Acts 17:10-11). Whenever Paul preached, the Bereans checked it out to see if Paul's teaching coincided with the scriptures. Whenever you hear the Word of God preached, regardless of who says it, realize that it must line up with what God says in His Word. Men and women are fallible, but God's Word can always be trusted. It is always the final authority. We need to study God's Word so we know the truth (2 Timothy 2:15).

REFLECTION
How do you know when you mind needs to be renewed? According to Ephesians 5:25-26, what does God use to cleanse us?

✱ The word "renew" means to make new & then new again over & ever repeatedly—so we always need renewed but when we start

✱ With washing with water thru the word of God.

appearance of the world—desperately need it desperately—Now it!

God's Word gives us power to live

Some years ago, a friend went to visit one of his neighbors who had been sick for a long time. The neighbor was in a subconscious state and couldn't respond to anyone who came into his room. My friend took his Bible along and began to read the Word of God. An amazing thing happened. For the first time in weeks, the man began to stir. The Word is full of living power...*whatever God says to us is full of living power (Hebrews 4:12 Living Bible)*.

Jesus realized that the key to His life was in knowing the Word of God and communing with His Father in Heaven. God has given us the Bible so that we can know the Word of God, apply it to our lives and defeat the devil. Taking time each day to commune with God and to read His Word protects us from the lies of the enemy. When Jesus was tempted in the wilderness, He said to the devil, in Matthew 4:4...*It is written: Man does not live on bread alone, but on every word that comes from the mouth of God.*

If I receive an email from a person, it is a direct communication from that person. When we read the Word of God, God speaks to us clearly. Jesus and His Word are one (John 1:2).

A common problem many Christians experience is finding time to read and meditate on the Word of God each day. The devil and the demons of hell will do everything they can to keep a Christian from studying the scriptures and communing with the Lord through His Word. God wants us to set aside a specific time to

DAY 6

pray and read His Word each day. Take that time seriously and plan for it. It will not just happen.

Reading a scripture with your bowl of cereal in the morning and then praying for two minutes as you drive to work or school does not really add up to a time of communing with Jesus! However, it is important to start somewhere. Start by reading a few verses each day and expect the Lord to speak to you. Take time to be with your friend, Jesus. As you grow in the Lord, you will want to spend more time with Him.

I have found that by reading one or two chapters from the New Testament and two or three chapters from the Old Testament each day, I can read through the entire Bible each year. But that is not where I started as a young Christian. I started with what I could handle—several minutes each day.

Those who do not spend time in the Word of God each day become weak. What happens if you do not eat food for a few days? You become physically weak. If we do not meditate on the Word each day, we become spiritually weak.

✻ It is FULL of power
living power.
✻ by feeding on the bread of life - the living
every
word of
God.

When we are born again and receive Jesus Christ through faith, our spirit has been reborn by the Spirit of God. Our soul, mind, will and emotions are being renewed each day by the Word of God as we meditate on His Word.

Meditate on God's Word

We need Jesus and His Word in our lives each day. Without Him, we can do absolutely nothing, but with Him, we can do all things (Philippians 4:13). Whenever I do not have the Word of God flowing through my life by daily prayerful study of the Word of God, I find myself growing weak spiritually. I cannot do the things that God has called me to do. Jesus promises in John 15:4-5, *remain in me, and I will remain in you. No branch can bear fruit by itself; it must remain in the vine. Neither can you bear fruit unless you remain in me. I am the vine; you are the branches. If a man remains in me and I in him, he will bear much fruit; apart from me you can do nothing.*

DAY 7

As we allow the life of God to come into us when we commune with Him daily by His Word, our lives will bear spiritual fruit. And that is exactly what the Lord has called us to do—bear fruit.

The Living Bible tells us, "the backslider gets bored with himself, but the godly man's life is exciting" (Proverbs 14:14). Our lives will be filled with excitement as we get to know God and experience His Word helping us overcome obstacles in our lives. People around us should say, "What do you have? I want it." As we meditate on the Word of God, He builds faith in our lives to do

REFLECTION

What qualities of Galatians 5:22-23 are produced in your life by meditating on God's Word?

what He has told us to do. We should meditate on His Word day and night. *But his delight is in the law of the Lord, and on his law he meditates day and night. He is like a tree planted by streams of water, which yields its fruit in season and whose leaf does not wither. Whatever he does prospers (Psalms 1:2-3).*

The word *meditate* literally means *to roll something around over and over again in our minds.* Memorizing the Word is a part of the meditating process. When you and I eat physical food, that food becomes bone, blood and tissue in our bodies. When we meditate on the Word of God, it spiritually becomes a part of our lives. We begin to act and react the way Jesus does because of the power that is in His Word. Those who live in the Word of God will produce spiritual fruit. The Bible says in Galatians 5:22-23, *But the fruit of the Spirit is love, joy, peace, patience, kindness, goodness, faithfulness, gentleness and self-control..*

All of the fruit of the Holy Spirit will become a very active part of our lives when we meditate on the Word of God each day and commune with Him. Are you meditating on God's Word each day? If not, today is your day to begin.

CHAPTER 2

Knowing God Through Prayer and Worship

KEY MEMORY VERSE

...true worshipers will worship the Father in spirit
and truth, for they are the kind of worshipers the
Father seeks. God is spirit, and his worshipers
must worship in spirit and in truth.
John 4:23-24

Prayer, our communication line with God

Besides meditating on God's Word, another way we can fellowship with the Lord each day is through prayer. The Lord wants to communicate with us! Ephesians 6:18 says, *And pray in the Spirit on all occasions with all kinds of prayers and requests. With this in mind, be alert and always keep on praying for all the saints.*

Prayer is our communication line with our God. During war, if a battalion loses contact with headquarters, the soldiers are in serious trouble, becoming much more vulnerable to the enemy. It often works the same way in our Christian lives. We are in a spiritual war. The devil is constantly trying to break down our communication line with God.

Prayer is only as complicated as we make it. God has not asked us to pray fancy prayers. Prayer is simply communication with Him. It is talking with God, sharing our hearts and listening. God wants us to talk to Him in the same way we talk to our closest friend. I often write down my prayers and then I can give praise to God when I see these prayers answered. When we know that God is answering prayer, it builds our faith.

Prayer can take various forms. We can pray in the language we speak (English, Spanish, Swahili, French, etc.) or speak in tongues (our prayer language between us and God used to build up our spiritual life). Paul is referring to both when he describes how he prays in 1 Corinthians 14:15...*I will pray with my spirit, but I will also pray with my mind....* ✳

Paul prayed with his spirit and he prayed with his mind. In other words, a believer can pray with his spirit (in tongues) as the Holy Spirit gives the utterance (1 Corinthians 12:7,11; Acts 2:4) or

REFLECTION

Describe prayer in your own words. According to 1 Corinthians 14:15, what two things can a believer pray with?

pray with his mind (in a known language) also under the impulse of the Holy Spirit.

When our spirits are praying in our heavenly language (in tongues), we are bypassing the devil by using a direct prayer line that God has given to us (1 Corinthians 14:2). It is equally important to pray prayers directed by God in our own language. Both are needed! (For more on praying in tongues, see Biblical Foundation 3, *New Testament Baptisms.*)

1. The intimate pouring out or emptying of oneself to the lover of our souls. A heavenly exchange

Lord, teach us to pray

Jesus lived a life-style of prayer. He was constantly in communication and fellowship with His Father in heaven. *But Jesus often withdrew to lonely places and prayed (Luke 5:16).*

...Jesus went out to a mountainside to pray, and spent the night praying to God (Luke 6:12).

The disciples witnessed Jesus' prayer life and wanted it for themselves. *One day Jesus was praying in a certain place. When he finished, one of his disciples said to him, "Lord, teach us to pray..." (Luke 11:1).*

To my knowledge, the only thing that the disciples actually asked Jesus to teach them was "to pray." They saw how Jesus prayed in secret. Whenever Jesus was involved with people, they saw miracles and wonderful events take place through Jesus' life and ministry. They knew there was a direct correlation between His communing with His Father and the supernatural occurrences. Jesus set the example of listening to the voice of the Holy Spirit to direct Him in every situation. His heavenly Father gave Him the ability to always know just where to go and who to talk and minister to.

John Wesley, the founder of the Methodist church, once said, "Give me one hundred preachers who fear nothing but sin and desire nothing but God, and I care not a straw whether they be clergymen or laymen, such alone will shake the gates of Hell and set up the kingdom of Heaven on earth. God does nothing but in answer to prayer." Wesley knew that God uses prayer in our lives to fulfill His purposes.

REFLECTION
Why did Jesus withdraw from the world to commune with God? Why did the disciples want to learn to pray as Jesus did?

* For direction & intimacy.
* they saw power modeled in prayer

A model prayer

Jesus gave His disciples a model prayer, which we call *The Lord's Prayer.* The purpose of this prayer was to teach us how to pray. Jesus said in Matthew 6:9-13, *in this manner, therefore, pray: Our Father in heaven, Hallowed be Your name. Your kingdom come. Your will be done On earth as it is in heaven. Give us this day our daily bread. And forgive us our debts, as we forgive our debtors. And do not lead us into temptation, but deliver us from the evil one.*

For Yours is the kingdom and the power and the glory forever. Amen (NKJ).

This prayer has helped me pray throughout nearly 35 years of walking with Jesus. When Jesus says, "Our Father in Heaven, hallowed be Your name," He is simply saying, "Father, Your name is holy. We lift up Your name."

Jesus declares, "Your kingdom come." We also should declare His kingdom to come and His will to be done on earth as it is in Heaven. We can declare that God's kingdom will come and His will be accomplished in our families, our communities, our church, our schools, our places of business, our small groups, and literally everywhere we go. When we pray, "Give us this day our daily bread," we are asking for the things that we need. God wants us to ask. He tells us that "we have not because we ask not" (James 4:2).

When Jesus prayed, "Forgive us our debts as we forgive our debtors," He reinforced the truth that we must forgive anyone who has sinned against us. If we do not forgive, God cannot forgive us (Matthew 6:14-15).

When we declare, "Do not lead us into temptation, but deliver us from the evil one," we are reminded of the truth that the Lord has called us to stand against the powers of darkness in Jesus' name. That is why the Word of God tells us we should resist the devil and he will flee from us (James 4:7).

Jesus closes this model prayer by declaring, "For Yours is the kingdom and the power and the glory forever. Amen." The Lord's Prayer starts and closes by giving honor and glory to our God through Jesus Christ. We can follow His example.

REFLECTION

What have you learned about prayer through studying this model?

[handwritten: It shows us how to praise God & to agree with Him that our relationship is of as Father to children & that we are to ask agreement with His will for His healing as we are in constant need of it forgiveness because we have no desire & require it. To come to receive forgiveness & blessing we in turn do & must do the act of forgiving & blessing. To ask Him to be our fortress in times of testing & weakness & to empower us against our common enemy who is satan not man.]

Let your requests be known

The Bible teaches us to pray without ceasing (1 Thessalonians 5:17). We need to be in a constant attitude of prayer all day long whether we are at work, home, school, or spending time with friends. We can pray on the way to the office or while cutting the grass. Jesus gives us this advice in Luke 11:9-10...*ask and it will be given to you; seek and you will find; knock and the door will be opened to you. For everyone who asks receives; he who seeks finds;*

20   Biblical Foundations

and to him who knocks, the door will be opened. If you lost a check with a whole week's wages, how long would you search for it? You probably would search until you found it. We need the same tenacity as we pray. We need to continue to ask and thank God for His answers until we experience an answer to our prayers. God may answer, "yes," "no," or "wait."

It amazes me how God will answer almost any prayer that a new Christian prays. When babies are born into a family, they get constant attention every time they cry. When they begin to grow up and mature, they do not always get their own way. As we begin to grow in the Lord, we may not always get our prayers answered the same way. The Lord wants to give us what is best for us, not always what we want.

God instructs us to refuse anxiety as we talk to Him and walk with Him in a constant attitude of thanksgiving. Philippians 4:6 tells us that we should...*not be anxious about anything, but in everything, by prayer and petition, with thanksgiving, present your requests to God.*

Several years ago, my family had a financial need. We were living on a very small budget and obeying God in every way that we knew. One day, I was praying for the Lord to provide for us financially. I opened the door of our home so that I could go to work and I saw the most amazing phenomenon. Money was all over the place! It was on the front lawn, the porch, and all around the house—even on the back lawn! You may ask, "How did it get there?" I have no idea. Did it ever happen again? No, but I will never forget it. All I know is that God did it, and it was a blessing to us. God is a supernatural God who answers prayers in a supernatural way.

> **REFLECTION**
> *What are three possible answers to our prayers? How can we eliminate anxiety from our lives, according to Philippians 4:6?*
> ⅄ Yes, No, wait.
> ✶ prayer, petition, gratitude

Praise and worship brings us to the Father

Fellowship with God not only includes meditating on His Word and praying but also *worshiping and praising* the Lord. To *praise* God means *to respond to God for what He has done.* Praise God for specific things He has done in your life.

Worship focuses more on *who God is*—on His person. We thank Him because He is God. Everyone worships something. Some people worship themselves. Some people worship their jobs, a motorcycle, sports or a spouse. We have been chosen to worship only God. The word *worship* comes from an old Anglo-Saxon word, *weorthsceipe*, which means *to ascribe worth to our God.* Only God is worthy of glory and praise. The Bible says in John 4:23-24 that we must worship with our heart, it cannot be merely form because *...true worshipers will worship the Father in spirit and truth, for they are the kind of worshipers the Father seeks. God is spirit, and his worshipers must worship in spirit and in truth.*

I must admit, I don't always feel like worshiping God. Praising or worshiping the Lord is not to be dependent upon our emotions, but instead a *decision* we make. God is worthy of all glory and praise. The Bible says that we should offer Him a sacrifice of praise. *Through Jesus, therefore, let us continually offer to God a sacrifice of praise—the fruit of lips that confess his name (Hebrews 13:15).*

The tabernacle of David in the Old Testament was known as a place of freedom in praise and worship. God is going to rebuild the tabernacle of David again in the last days (Acts 15:16). That is why God is bringing the freedom to worship to His church today.

Music is a basic form of worship. Music was so important in David's day that he appointed people with instruments to praise and worship the Lord (1 Chronicles 15:16;16:5-6). God is restoring praise and worship to His church today. God's original intention of unbridled praise and worship will be restored to His church.

We need to be involved privately in praise and worship to our God in our time alone with Him. In the same way that the moon reflects the glory of the sun, we will reflect the glory of God in our lives as we spend time worshiping Him. The book of Psalms is filled with songs of praise to our God. I encourage you to take the book of Psalms and begin to sing those

REFLECTION
Explain the difference between praise and worship. What is a true worshiper, according to John 4:23-24?

psalms and make up your own songs and to use them to give worship to God.

✝ praise is gratitude for what He has done
✝ worship is exaltation for who He is.
✝ A reflection of Him.

He is worthy to receive praise

Heaven is a place that will be filled with praise and worship! Revelation 5:11-12 describes a scene of heaven. *Then I looked and heard the voice of many angels...They encircled the throne and the living creatures and the elders. In a loud voice they sang: Worthy is the Lamb, who was slain, to receive power and wealth and wisdom and strength and honor and glory and praise!*

Some people think that worship should be quiet. There is a place for quietly worshiping God, but the Bible also encourages us to worship God with a loud voice (Psalm 47:1). You can go to a football game and see thousands of people get emotionally charged by a little pigskin being thrown around a field. Think how much more exciting it is because Jesus Christ went to the cross and gave His life for you! That's why we shout unto God and praise and bless Him—He is worthy to receive the praise due only to Him!

We worship God here on earth in preparation for heaven. I certainly do not want to be a spiritually dead person who cannot praise the Lord. *It is not the dead who praise the Lord, those who go down to silence (Psalms 115:17).*

Although I am not an exceptionally emotional person, when I realize what Jesus Christ did for me, my spirit, soul, and body begins to get caught up in praise and worship to my God. According to the scripture, the demons of hell can be bound (tied up spiritually) through praise and worship to our God. Psalms 149:6-8 says, *May the praise of God be in their mouths and a double-edged sword in their hands, to inflict vengeance on the nations and punishment on the peoples, to bind their kings with fetters, their nobles with shackles of iron.*

Whether we are alone or with two or three others or with one thousand people, the demons tremble when God's people commune with Him through praise and worship.

REFLECTION
What happens when we praise God, according to Psalms 149:6-8? How does God live in our praises?

God inhabits, actually lives in, the praises of His people. *But You are holy, who inhabit the praises of Israel (Psalms 22:3 NKJ).*

He strengthens us, vindicates + rescues us. He also sides with us to side with Him

In holiness + power

Expressing worship

There are many ways that we can express worship and praise to our God. Here are just a few of the ways mentioned in the scriptures. First of all, we can kneel before the Lord. *Come, let us bow down in worship, let us kneel before the Lord our Maker (Psalms 95:6).* We can stand and worship our God like the multitude of people in Revelation 7:9-10. *A great multitude that no one could count, from every nation, tribe, people and language, standing before the throne and in front of the Lamb. They were wearing white robes and were holding palm branches in their hands. And they cried out in a loud voice: "Salvation belongs to our God, who sits on the throne, and to the Lamb."*

The scripture also says there are times God has called us to lift up our hands to the Lord. *I want men everywhere to lift up holy hands in prayer...(1 Timothy 2:8).*

Other scriptures teach us we should be still before the Lord. *Be still, and know that I am God...(Psalms 46:10).*

We are also exhorted to praise Him with instruments. *Praise him with the sounding of the trumpet, praise him with the harp and lyre...praise him with the clash of cymbals, praise him with resounding cymbals (Psalms 150:3,5).*

We can also worship the Lord in dance. The word *dance* in Hebrew means *the lifting of the feet.* David danced before the Lord in the Old Testament. The devil has taken the dance and made it sensual, but God is restoring dance to His church in purity through praise and worship to our King Jesus. Psalms 149:3 says, *Let them praise his name with dancing and make music to him with tambourine and harp.*

God has also called us to sing new songs to our God. Singing a new song is simply asking God to give us a tune or a melody and then allowing the Holy Spirit to give us the words. Or we can take the words directly from the scriptures and sing them to Him. *Praise the Lord. Sing to the Lord a new song, his praise in the assembly of the saints (Psalms 149:1).*

The scripture also speaks of clapping and shouting unto the Lord. Remember the time God's people marched around Jericho day after day? On the seventh day, the walls came tumbling down. Demons tremble when we shout because of what Jesus Christ has done and because of who He is. The Bible says we should clap and shout with cries of joy. *Clap your hands, all you nations; shout to God with cries of joy* (Psalms 47:1).

Ephesians 5:19 says that we should be speaking to one another in psalms and hymns and spiritual songs and making melody in our hearts to the Lord. When a couple gets married, the greatest desire they have is to be in a relationship together, to spend time together. This involves both speaking and listening. Our God wants us to have communion with Him and relationship with Him. Sometimes we express that relationship by being quiet and listening. Sometimes we shout unto our God. Other times we talk or weep. We've been created to praise and commune with our wonderful, heavenly Daddy.

REFLECTION

List the physical ways we can express our worship to God. How many do you use when worshiping God?

1. kneeling
2. standing + worship
3. raising of hands
4. being still
5. instruments
6. dance
7. singing
8. Clapping + sings
9. speaking listening + choring God

CHAPTER 3

How Can We Hear God's Voice?

KEY MEMORY VERSE
Trust in the Lord with all your heart and
lean not on your own understanding;
in all your ways acknowledge him,
and he will make your paths straight.
Proverbs 3:5-6

"Is that you, God?"

One evening after I taught at a church, a young man came to me and shared his struggle. "I feel the Lord is calling me to go to the mission field, but I'm not sure if I should quit my job or not. I keep hearing different voices. How do I know whether or not I am hearing God's voice clearly?"

Another time, a young man in his late teens stopped by our house and declared he had heard God's voice. He had a strange expression on his face and then spelled it out. "The Lord spoke to me today...and He told me to kill myself." I was momentarily stunned! But I knew from the Word of God the Lord would never tell someone to kill himself. It was clear the young man was hearing some other voice.

One time I was driving down a rural road when I passed a hitchhiker. I sensed a voice telling me to go back and pick him up. I thought the Lord wanted me to share my faith with him. When I turned around, he was nowhere in sight. I was confused. I thought the Lord had spoken to me.

Christians sometimes find themselves in situations where they struggle to hear God's voice. We really want to do what the Lord wants us to do. We know that we serve a living God who wants to speak to us, and yet we struggle with the fact that we often do not hear as clearly as we would like to. Sometimes we may think we have heard the Lord's voice and respond to it, only to find out that we were wrong. Instead of pressing in to find out why we "missed it," we hesitate to step out in faith the next time. Other times, we get so involved in the affairs of this natural world that we forget to listen to the voice of the Lord and receive His instructions for our daily living.

REFLECTION
Why did Jesus have to speak often with His heavenly Father (John 8:29)?
Have you ever obeyed what you thought was God's voice and later found it was not? Explain.

You probably know this already, but the Lord does not speak to us in reverb. Granted, in the movie, *The Ten Commandments*, the Lord spoke to Moses in a deep, booming voice, but that was only sound effects! How does He really speak to us? How can we hear His voice? 1. because He cared what His Father had to say + desired His Guidance.

2. of course - Give away $ to this or that + I am a steward.

Biblical Foundations

Let's see what God's Word says about hearing His voice. One day, Jesus made an interesting statement, *The one who sent me is with me; he has not left me alone, for I always do what pleases him (John 8:29).*

Jesus does only what the Father in heaven has told Him to do. If it is important for Jesus to hear from His Father in heaven, how much more important is it for each of us to hear His voice clearly? Read on to discover how to hear God's voice more clearly.

Acknowledge God's voice

For those who are willing to check in with their heavenly Father about decisions of life, Proverbs 3:5-6 promises, *Trust in the Lord with all your heart and lean not on your own understanding; in all your ways acknowledge him, and he will make your paths straight.*

After serving the Lord for more than three decades, I am totally convinced that it is a whole lot harder to get out of His will than we think. If we do get off course, He will reach out in love and nudge us back on track, if we are really trusting and acknowledging Him in our lives.

What does *acknowledge* mean? The Webster dictionary says it is *to admit the existence, reality, or truth of or express gratitude for.* So then, if we acknowledge a new friend, we talk to him, express our appreciation for him, and recognize his presence in our lives.

Imagine your friends not acknowledging your presence when you are together. You try to talk to them, and they completely ignore you. In fact, they talk right over you as if you were not even there. That is how we treat the Lord if we are not acknowledging Him moment by moment in our lives. If we are not recognizing His presence in our lives, we are probably not hearing the voice of the Lord as we should.

The Lord desires to speak to us in many ways, and we need to allow Him to do so. I spend much of my time traveling throughout the world teaching the Bible. One of the things that I miss most when I travel is communicating with my family. I really miss spending time with my wife, LaVerne. However, because of the technologically advanced age we live in, I can usually communicate with her regardless of where I am in the world. I don't care whether the message comes by phone, fax, email, letter, or by a note. I just want to hear from her.

Let's not get too selective about how the Lord speaks to us. We need to get to a place where we want to hear His voice desperately. This desire comes out of a love relationship with Him. The Lord may speak to us at times in dreams, visions, or by His audible voice, but these are not the ways that He usually speaks to us. Usually, the Lord speaks to us either by His Word or by His Spirit speaking to our spirits. Jesus tells us that if we continue in His Word, we shall know the truth...*If you hold to my teaching, you are really my disciples. Then you will know the truth, and the truth will set you free (John 8:31-32).* He speaks to us by His Word! We will never go off track if we obey the Word of God!

REFLECTION

What happens when we acknowledge God (Proverbs 3:5-6)? How does God give us truth and how does it set us free (John 8:31-32)?

God's voice is compatible with God's Word!

We need to saturate ourselves with God's Word. We must have a full reservoir of the Word of God to draw from so we do not become deceived by the enemy. Any dream, prophecy, vision or audible voice that does not line up with scripture is not the voice of God. Scripture is given as a standard so that we will never get off track. 2 Timothy 3:16-17 describes God's Word this way, *All Scripture is God-breathed and is useful for teaching, rebuking, correcting and training in righteousness, so that the man of God may be thoroughly equipped for every good work.*

A man asked me one time if I could give my "stamp of approval" on his decision to divorce his wife and marry another woman in the church whom he felt could be more compatible with him in his ministry. I told him that no matter how right it felt to him, his plan was in direct disobedience to the Lord. How did I know? I knew from the scriptures, in Mark 10:11-12, that he would be committing adultery.

If we want to mature in our Christian lives, we will learn to renew our minds with God's Word so we can distinguish between good and evil. We will practice doing right. *You will never be able to eat solid spiritual food and understand the deeper things of God's*

1. He will give you a clear understanding + reassurance of blessing + peace of mind in the direction your life is headed.

30

2. Freedom is the proving result that His word is indeed true.

Word until you become better Christians and learn right from wrong by practicing doing right (Hebrews 5:12-14, Living Bible).

God's Word never changes. Many times, however, the area in which we need guidance is not in direct conflict with the scriptures. We may need to know the answers for some of the following questions: What is the Lord's plan for my career? Do I need to consider further training? Where should I live? Should I buy a house or a car? Where should I go to college? Which group of believers has the Lord called me to serve with? This is the time to learn to listen to the voice of the Holy Spirit speaking to our spirits.

REFLECTION
What is the first step in determining if some thought or word is from God (2 Timothy 3:16-17)? How does God's Word benefit you (Hebrews 5:12-14)?

1. check with scripture.
2. It is consistant + so is the resulting blessing benefit.

Allow the Holy Spirit to enlighten your spirit

The Lord desires to speak to us by His Spirit. Romans 8:16 says, *The Spirit himself testifies with our spirit that we are God's children.* Proverbs 20:27 says, *The lamp of the Lord searches the spirit of a man; it searches out his inmost being.*

Your spirit along with your soul dwell inside your body. Your spirit and soul live forever. Your soul includes your mind, will and emotions and your spirit communicates with the Holy Spirit.

We are learning on this earth how we can communicate with the Holy Spirit. Many times, we hear a voice deep within us but excuse it as "just us." The Lord wants to teach us to trust the Holy Spirit to speak to our spirit. Our spirit is like a lamp that the Lord will "light" and use to give us clear direction.

We often think that hearing God's voice is complicated. It is really not as hard as we think. When my wife and I were preparing to become missionaries as a young couple, we had two choices. Our mission board told us there was an opening in the states of Connecticut and South Carolina. As we prayed, the Lord placed a burden on our hearts for the people on an island off the coast of South Carolina. We didn't hear God speak in an audible voice, but the feeling kept getting stronger. We knew it was the right place.

We need to expect an answer from the Lord when we are really serious about listening to Him. The scriptures tell us, *In his heart a man plans his course, but the Lord determines his steps (Proverbs*

DAY 4

16:9). Look back at your life and see how the Lord has directed your steps. Sometimes God speaks to us by putting a desire or burden in our hearts that we know would not be from anyone else but God.

You can trust God. He speaks to those whose trust is completely in Him. As a boy growing up, I trapped muskrats every winter. Early every morning before dawn, I would follow the trap line to inspect my traps. Whenever I saw moving shadows or heard strange sounds, I would freeze in my tracks with fear. On those dark, cold, wintery mornings, the most comforting sound I could hear was the voice of my father, who would finish his morning chores and meet me on the trap line. Just the sound of his voice calling my name gave me a sense of peace and security.

Jesus is teaching us to hear His voice. He tells us, in John 10:4, that the sheep hear the shepherd's voice. *When he has brought out all his own, he goes on ahead of them, and his sheep follow him because they know his voice.* There are various voices that the sheep hear; however, they will not follow the voice of a stranger. The sheep have been trained to only follow the voice of the shepherd.

R E F L E C T I O N
What are some ways the Lord has spoken to you through he Holy Spirit? Do you always recognize the voice of your Shepherd?

Beware of other voices

When I first became a Christian, I thought that, from that day on, I was only going to hear the voice of God. Wow, was I ever in for a shock! I actually heard all kinds of voices inside my head. I soon realized that some of those voices most certainly were not the voice of the Holy Spirit. As time went on, experience taught me that there are at least four different kinds of voices a person may hear. If we are not hearing God's voice, we are hearing our own voice, the voice of others, or even the devil's voice at times. How can we know which voice is resounding inside of us?

Our own voice Let's talk about our own voice first. Remember, our soul is our mind, will and emotions. So, then, the decisions that we often want to make originate from our beliefs, which are manifested in our feelings and emotions. This includes our personal preferences and desires, such as whether or not we like pizza, who our favorite football team is, or if we like shopping, deer hunting or cherry pie. These things are not wrong, but they are personal preferences, not the voice of God. Many times, Christians confuse their own desires with the voice of the Lord.

Other people's voices Instead of God's voice, we may also hear other people's voices vying for our attention. 2 Corinthians 10:5 tells us, *We demolish arguments and every pretension that sets itself up against the knowledge of God, and we take captive every thought to make it obedient to Christ.*

Many times, the voices we hear have been placed inside us by those who try to sell us their products or philosophies. Whenever these thoughts and opinions are hostile to the Word of God, we are told to demolish them.

REFLECTION
How do we "take captive every thought to make it obedient to Christ"?

Sometimes it is difficult to know if we have heard from God correctly and to know if others have also heard correctly. We are told in 1 John 4:1 to test the "spirits." If another believer speaks out a word from God for you, test it. Ask God to confirm to you if this is really from Him. If you have any doubts, go to your pastor or other Christian leader. Ask them to pray about it with you.

Enemy talk vs. the still small voice

The voice of the enemy A third voice that we may hear instead of God's voice is the voice of the enemy. The devil does not appear to us in a red jumpsuit with a long tail. He comes very slyly as an angel of light (2 Corinthians 11:14). He may use well-meaning people to speak words that could water down our faith. Or, he could place thoughts into our minds that are contrary to God's Word.

How often have you decided to get serious about studying the scriptures and a voice informs you that there are chores that need to be completed immediately? Tell the devil the same thing that Jesus told him, "It is written." Resist him in Jesus' name, and he will flee!

For a time in my life, while driving in my car, the enemy would attempt to place a cloud of depression around me. One day, I boldly spoke the Word to myself and the powers of darkness in the car. I shouted...*the one who is in [me] is greater than the one who is in the world (1 John 4:4).* Within minutes, the whole atmosphere in the car changed. The presence of the Lord replaced the presence of the enemy. I had silenced the enemy's voice by proclaiming the truth of the Word of God.

The voice of God The real voice we want to hear and obey is the voice of our God speaking to our spirit. We often call the Lord's voice a "still, small voice." This phrase comes from the story of Elijah in 1 Kings 19:11-13, when God spoke to him in a "still, small voice." Often, we are looking for the Lord to speak to us in an earth-shattering way. But the Lord usually speaks to us by His Spirit, deep within our spirits.

Psalm 46:10 says, *Be still and know that I am God.* It is important to take time to be quiet and listen. If you get together with a close friend and do all the talking without listening, the relationship is one-sided. In our prayers, we should talk to God, but we need to listen, too.

Most of the major decisions in my life have come as a result of that "still, small voice." When the Lord spoke to me about being involved in church planting through small groups, He asked,

REFLECTION
Name some ways you resist the devil and his lies.
Give examples of times God led you by His still, small voice.

"Are you willing to be involved in the underground church?" It was not a booming voice in an earthquake, but a "still, small voice." The "voice" was very clear—it changed the direction of my life.

There are times when I am picking up something for my family at the grocery store and a "still, small voice" tells me to purchase an extra item, not on the list. Nearly always, when I get home, the item that I chose was needed. If we are sensitive to the Holy Spirit, we will hear when He speaks. On one occasion, the Holy Spirit asked me to give some money to a missionary family. I was later informed that they had no money for food, and this gift was an answer to their prayers.

Ask God to communicate to you during your times with Him, and all throughout the day. You will learn more and more to discern what is your voice and what is the Holy Spirit's. You will learn how to hear the voice of God and obey Him.

Tuning in to God's voice

Did you ever experience a verse almost leaping off the pages of the Bible? You may have read it one thousand times, but this time it really "grabs" you. God is speaking to you!

A husband may be relaxing and feel impressed to help his wife with some of the maintenance around the house. He should not be too quick to rebuke that thought! It is probably the Lord speaking to him. A teenager is listening to her favorite CD or talking to one of her friends on the telephone. A voice inside tells her to clean her room. It is probably God!

We learn to hear the voice of the Lord through practice and obedience. Sometimes we may feel discouraged trying to discern between the Lord's voice, the enemy's voice, others' voices, and our own voice. Sometimes it seems like we are listening to a radio station with a weak signal, while a few other stations continue to fade in and out. But, as we continue to listen to the voice of our Shepherd, we will learn the difference between the voices.

Loren Cunningham, the founder of *Youth With A Mission,* says that he has found three simple steps that have helped him and thousands of YWAMers to hear God's voice:

SUBMIT to His Lordship. Ask Him to help you silence your own thoughts, desires, and the opinions of others which may be filling your mind (2 Corinthians 10:5). Even though you have been given a good mind to use, you want to hear the thoughts of the Lord who has the best mind (Proverbs 3:5-6).

RESIST the enemy in case he is trying to deceive you. Use the authority that Jesus Christ has given you to silence the voice of the enemy (James 4:7; Ephesians 6:10-20).

EXPECT an answer. After asking the question that is on your mind, wait for Him to answer. Expect your loving heavenly father to speak to you, and He will (John 10:27; Psalms 69:13; Exodus 33:11).

REFLECTION

Remember some times when you had to discern between your own voice, the voice of others, the voice of the enemy, and the voice of the Lord. What can you learn from your past that will keep you from making the same mistakes in the future?

Years ago, we were at a shopping mall with our two younger children. In one split second our then four-year-old daughter was missing from view. I instantly called out her name. Thankfully, she quickly responded to the voice of her father. I was so relieved to see her! Our heavenly Father wants His children to heed His voice. *Lord, teach us to hear Your voice and to obey it.*

CHAPTER 4

Hearing His Voice Clearly

KEY MEMORY VERSE

...Do not let this Book of the Law depart from your mouth; meditate on it day and night, so that you may be careful to do everything written in it. Then you will be prosperous and successful.

Joshua 1:8

The struggle to stay on track

Sometimes hearing the voice of the Lord is like driving down the road through intense fog late at night. It is really a struggle. The painted line in the center is our guide, and if we can see a car in front of us, we can follow its taillights. The painted line in the center of the road is symbolic of the Word of God. The most basic way that God speaks is through His Word, and we cannot go wrong by following it. The taillights from the car that we are following are symbolic of the Holy Spirit who guides us and helps us to stay on track.

There are times, however, when it seems like we have entirely lost our way. We really want to obey the Lord and fulfill His will for our lives, but somehow we can no longer see the taillights of the car in front of us or the painted line on the road. What do we do then? There is a story in the Old Testament that gives us some insight. A man was cutting down a tree by the river when his iron ax head fell into the water. An ax head was a very expensive tool, and the man desperately wanted to retrieve it because it was borrowed. He went to Elisha, a man of God, for help. Elisha asked where he had last seen it fall, threw a stick in the water, and it miraculously floated to the surface! (2 Kings 6:1-6). At the same place that it was lost, the ax head reappeared!

We can learn an important lesson from this. Whenever we have problems with finding direction in our lives, it is often helpful to go back to where we were certain we last heard the voice of the Lord clearly. If we do not go back, we may continue to flounder and be distressed. If we believe that we've lost our way spiritually, the Bible is very clear...*Remember the height from which you have fallen! Repent and do the things you did at first...(Revelation 2:5).*

We must go back to where the ax head fell, and remember the "height from which we have fallen"—where our love and obedience for the Lord declined. We need to acknowledge the Lord when we get off track and then repent (turn around) and go back to the last time we heard the clear, sharp, cutting-edge voice of the Lord. Then obey.

REFLECTION
Give examples of "ax heads" in your Christian walk. What does Revelation 2:5 advise us to do?

[handwritten notes] 1. Pushing past God losing my way & making things "personal" — more about me than Him. Remember where we fail from & repent + go back to those I & love things we did at 1st

The Lord called a young man to go far from home to a Bible school. After spending a few weeks in the school, he found himself having second thoughts about his decision. He hated the discipline, the climate—you name it. He stayed, however, when he remembered the time the Lord had clearly called him to go to that school. By being obedient, he was a recipient of the benefits, and the Lord did a tremendous work in His life.

Go back to where you lost your way

In 1992, I began to question whether or not I was called to church leadership. Anything else looked much better than to continue on in a leadership role. However, I remembered the initial call when God called me to start a new church in 1980. This was the place the ax head had fallen for me, and I was convinced the Lord had spoken to me and given me a mandate to start the church. Knowing this gave me the confidence to go on. I knew He had not yet completed the work He had begun.

Do you get tired of your job sometimes? Perhaps you are tired of going to school or of your involvement in the church. Go back to the last time you knew you heard clearly from the Lord on the subject, and allow the Lord to take you from there. If you made a mistake, there is hope. That is why Jesus came in the first place, to forgive us as we acknowledge our sin and cleanse us and give us a brand-new start.

Remember Jonah? He refused to obey the Lord, who told him to preach the gospel in the city of Nineveh. God got his attention by using ungodly sailors to push him into the ocean, and the Lord prepared a great fish to swallow him alive to give him some time to think. I believe Jonah thought back to where "the ax head fell" (he went off-track) and quickly repented! The Lord gave him another chance and the fish spit him out on dry land. The Bible says in Jonah 3:1, *Then the word of the Lord came to Jonah a second time: "Go to the great city of Nineveh and proclaim to it the message I give you." Jonah obeyed the word of the Lord and went to Nineveh (Jonah 3:1-3a).*

As we repent before God, we can receive the word of the Lord a second time. A key question to ask ourselves is this, "Have I obeyed the last thing the Lord asked me to do?"

One thing that used to cause stress in our marriage was the fact that I was constantly trying to find shortcuts whenever my wife, LaVerne, and I were driving somewhere. To make matters worse, I usually got lost! To backtrack over and over again was embarrassing! I usually needed to go back to the last road I was familiar with before I could find the way.

REFLECTION

Have you had an experience where you struggled to repent, like Jonah? What did you do? What should you have done?

If you find yourself on the wrong path, it is not the end of the world. The Lord is able to "restore the years that the locusts have eaten" (Joel 2:25), but going back to the place where we last heard from God is often the way to get to our destination.

The Word of God should "align"

I learned a principle from a man of God once that has helped steer me in the right direction as I have attempted to hear God's voice. This man told a story of three lighthouses that were built to warn ships of the monstrous rocks which were below the surface of the water as they sailed into the harbor. To avoid getting snagged on these huge rocks, the captain had to be sure that the three lighthouses were aligned as he sailed into the harbor. If the captain could see two or three lighthouses at the same time, he knew he was in the danger zone.

In order to avoid shipwreck in our lives, we need to be sure that three different "lighthouses" are aligned before we begin to move in a new direction.

The first lighthouse to align is the Word of God. There is no substitute for God's Word. Paul, the apostle, tells us in 1 Corinthians 14:37, *If anyone thinks himself to be a prophet or spiritual, let him acknowledge that the things which I write to you are the commandments of the Lord.* God told Joshua in Joshua 1:8 to be faithful to God's Word. *Do not let this Book of the Law depart from your mouth; meditate on it day and night, so that you may be careful to do everything written in it. Then you will be prosperous and successful.*

When we obey the Word of God, we are promised to have good success. When we disobey the Word of God, it will cause shipwreck

1. Yes, but I wandered my own way rationalizing it until God disciplined me harshly. I should have repented + stayed out where I know my better interest was held.

in our lives. Things may be okay for a period of time, but eventually disobedience to God's Word will take a toll on our lives.

If anyone claims to have supernatural revelation from God, it must line up with the Word of God. The whole Mormon cult was started by Joseph Smith, a man who claimed he had a visitation from an angel. We know this was really a fallen angel or demonic spiritual being, because the message did not line up with the Word of God. It was a perversion of the true gospel. Paul, the apostle, urges the Galatian believers to not be persuaded by false teachers in Galatians 1:6-8. *I am astonished that you are so quickly deserting the one who called you by the grace of Christ and are turning to a different gospel—which is really no gospel at all.* Evidently some people are throwing you into confusion and are trying to pervert the gospel of Christ. But even if we or an angel from heaven should preach a gospel other than the one we preached to you, let him be eternally condemned!

REFLECTION
What are we promised if we obey God's Word (Joshua 1:8)? What happens if we listen to something other than God's Word for direction?

Remember, the Bible says Satan comes to us like an angel of light (2 Corinthians 11:14). Check everything against the Word of God. If you are not sure, go to a mature believer or leader of your church. The Word of God is our standard to be sure that the revelation we are getting is in line with the perfect will of God. *1. Prosperity, success. 2. We could be chastised or ultimately condemned.*

The peace of God should "align"

The second spiritual lighthouse that needs to line up is the peace of God. The scriptures tell us in Colossians 3:15, *Let the peace of Christ rule in your hearts, since as members of one body you were called to peace. And be thankful.* The word *rule* literally means *to be an umpire.* In other words, the peace of God in our hearts is an umpire to alert us as to whether or not we should make a certain decision.

A man was offered a job by a large company where he would make much more money than he ever made in his life. He thought of all the wonderful things he could do with the money—use it to help friends who needed to buy an apartment, give money to the poor, help the homeless. However, he did not have peace from God about taking the job, so he turned it down. The president of the company thought he was crazy, as did some friends. It seemed like a once in a lifetime opportunity. But He could not take it without the blessing of God. A short time later, he found out that the president of the company had done many illegal things, and the whole company was in trouble. If he had taken the job, he might have been implicated just because he worked there. At the very least, he would

REFLECTION
How does the "peace of God" feel and how does it affect your life?

have had to choose between being honest and keeping the job. God kept this man from getting involved in a very messy situation.

Several years ago, a friend told me he wanted to give me his car. It was a beautiful car, but my wife, LaVerne, and I did not have the peace of God in our hearts to receive it. So we graciously declined. Some time later, the Lord provided our family with a van, and this time we had the peace to receive it from the benefactor. Obeying the peace of God in our hearts allows us to carry on with a sense of His acceptance and favor in our lives. *A calm assurance that all is ok lining up with confirmation w/out wrestling in your spirit Just peace. no heaviness.*

Circumstances should "align"

The third lighthouse to align is *circumstances*. Sometimes we can be so sure that something is God's will, but it is not the right timing for us. If you feel this way, it is best to let the desire die. If it is really from God, He will resurrect it (bring it back to life) in the future when the timing is right.

We have counseled countless young men and women who were sure the Lord had shown them whom they should marry, but the other person wasn't getting the same message. Our advice is to let the desire die for now, and if the Lord has really spoken it to you, it will happen sometime in the future.

If you believe the Lord wants you to buy a certain house or car, and it is not available, either you have missed the timing or it is not the Lord's answer for you. Timing is so important. You may have the right *direction* from the Lord, but the wrong *timing* as you try to fulfill it. Moses had the right vision from the Lord—deliver the Lord's people from the slavery of the Egyptians. The only problem—he initially missed the timing of God (by forty years!) when he killed an Egyptian. Someone may feel called to start a business or be a missionary, and the vision is a genuine vision from the Lord. Often the problem comes when they jump into it too fast. When the Lord is in it, the circumstances will work out.

The Lord clearly opened up a door for Paul in 1 Corinthians 16:8-9. The circumstances lined up with the Word of God and with the peace of God. Although Paul faced many adversaries, he knew that the Lord had opened up the door for him. *But I will stay on at Ephesus until Pentecost, because a great door for effective work has opened to me, and there are many who oppose me.*

Jeremiah gives an interesting account of heeding the voice of the Lord through circumstances. *Then this message from the Lord came to Jeremiah: "Your cousin Hanamel (son of Shallum) will soon arrive to ask you to buy the farm he owns in Anathoth, for by law you have a chance to buy before it is offered to anyone else." So, Hanamel came, as the Lord had said he would, and visited me in the prison. "Buy my field in Anathoth, in the land of Benjamin," he said, "for the law gives you the first right to purchase it." Then I knew for sure that the message I had heard was really from the Lord (Jeremiah 32:6-8, Living Bible).* After the circumstances lined up, Jeremiah knew that the message was from the Lord. If the Lord is asking you to do something, He will make it clear. You can trust Him.

REFLECTION
Describe a situation when you had the right direction from the Lord but missed His perfect timing. How did you know?

[handwritten: Kate the circumstance that could've been better prepared had I waited led]

DAY 6

God will make it clear

George Mueller was a man of faith from Bristol, England, who fed hundreds of children in his orphanages in 19th-century England. The following relates his valuable insights on hearing from God:

"I seek at the beginning to get my heart in such a state that it has no will of its own in regard to a given matter. Nine-tenths of the trouble with people generally is just there. Nine-tenths of the difficulties are overcome when our hearts are ready to do the Lord's will whatever it may be. When one is truly in this state, it is usually but a little way to the knowledge of what His will is.

"Having done this, I do not leave the result to feeling or simple impression. If so, I make myself liable to great delusions.

"I will seek the will of the Spirit of God through, or in connection with, the Word of God. The Spirit and the Word must be combined. If I look to the Spirit alone without the Word, I lay myself open to great delusions also. If the Holy Ghost guides us at all, He will do it according to the scriptures and never contrary to them.

"Next, I take into account providential circumstances. These often plainly indicate God's will in connection with His Word and Spirit.

"I ask God in prayer to reveal His will to me aright.

"Thus, through prayer to God, the study of the Word, and reflection, I come to deliberate judgment according to the best of my ability and knowledge, and if my mind is thus at peace, and continues so after two or three more petitions, I proceed accordingly. In trivial matters and in transactions involving most important issues, I find this method always effective.[1]

REFLECTION

What does George Mueller mean by "the Spirit and the Word must be combined"?

"I never remember, in all of my Christian course, a period now (in March 1895) of sixty-nine years and four months, that I ever sincerely and patiently sought to know the will of God by the teaching of the Holy Ghost, through the instrumentality of the Word of God, but I have always been directed rightly. But if honesty of heart and uprightness before God were lacking, or if I did not patiently wait upon God for instruction, or if I preferred the counsel of my fellow man to the declarations of the Word of the living God, I made great mistakes."[2]

That is good advice. Let us look for the three lighthouse beacon lights (the Word of God, the peace of God, and circumstances) to line up in the days ahead. If the lights do not line up, we are in danger of running into the rocks. I'm heading for the three beacon lights. How about you?

[1] *Answers to Prayer from George Mueller's Narratives,* Compiled by A.E.C. Brooks.
[2] From the classic biography of George Mueller, *George Müller of Bristol,* by A. T. Pierson.

Listen and communicate!

My wife, LaVerne, has learned years ago the importance of communing with God and having a real love relationship with her Father in Heaven. Sometime back, she shared these thoughts with a group of believers:

x If a person is led of God then if checked
& confirmed by ~~word~~ scripture
that life or act should take on the very nature,
attributes & patterns of God that He has set in
scripture as to be Holy,

"We as a church are engaged to Jesus, the bridegroom who is coming back for us—the bride. What do engaged couples do to have an effective relationship? They spend time together, not just talking, but listening to each other's heart, sharing each other's dreams. As they listen and talk together, they understand each other. If they just talk and do not listen, they have an ineffective relationship. So it is in our relationship with Jesus. It is Jesus' desire that we listen to Him and commune with Him. We need to see that we are engaged to Him and the Word of God needs to be powerful in our lives. When

REFLECTION
Describe the relationship Jesus desires to have with His bride—the church. Describe your relationship with Jesus. Ask someone to pray with you to have a more intimate relationship with Jesus.

the Word of God is in us, we understand and know who God is. We understand that He wants to speak to us. The Word of God is spirit and life within us. As we drive down the road, as we wash dishes, as we sit at the desk, we are aware of His presence and are willing to listen to that 'still, small voice' based on the Word of God, because the Word of God is in us. God desires to speak to us all day long. It is up to us to listen to Him."

Just as a husband and wife learn to communicate and have fellowship with one another and grow in their love relationship, the Lord teaches us to grow in our love relationship with Him. Jesus, our bridegroom, is coming back for us. Nothing is more important or has more eternal significance. *Husbands, love your wives, just as Christ loved the church and gave himself up for her to make her holy, cleansing her by the washing with water through the word, and to present her to himself as a radiant church, without stain or wrinkle or any other blemish, but holy and blameless (Ephesians 5:25-27).*

Jesus gave His life for us on the cross two thousand years ago. He paid the price for us to experience a loving relationship with our heavenly Father. He desires to guide and lead us as we build a relationship with Him. He is worthy of our fellowship and of our worship.

Knowing God Through His Word

1. How can we get to know such an awesome God?

a. God has made Himself known through Jesus Christ. John 17:3

b. God is one God (Mark 12:29).

2. When three equals one

a. God is one God who is three persons (Matthew 28:19).

b. God the Father, God the Son and God the Holy Spirit are coequal, coeternal members—three distinct persons who share a divine nature.

   Ex: Water takes on three forms: liquid, vapor and ice.

c. No one can fully explain God, but we can know Him by faith. Hebrews 11:6

3. Jesus is God

a. Some say Jesus was just a good man or a prophet.

b. Jesus boldly claimed to be God and the religious leaders were furious (John 10:24-38).

c. We can be certain Jesus is who He says He is. We are sure of this by His fulfillment of scripture, His sonship, His actions, the miracles He performed, and greatest of all—He rose from the dead!

4. God's Word is life to us

a. God invites us to know Him (Revelation 3:20).

b. We start to build a relationship by meditating on the Word of God (John 6:63).

   Ex: Evangelist Billy Graham advises: get to know God through His Word.

c. Jesus and His Word are one (John 1:1).

5. God's Word renews our minds

a. The world's system is one of selfishness and subject to the devil's rule (2 Corinthians 4:4). We cannot be conformed to this world's system (Romans 12:2).

   Ex: If we do not separate from the world, we become molded, like gelatin, to the world.

b. The Word of God cleanses us (Ephesians 5:25-26).

c. Always check that the Word of God lines up with what you hear preached (Acts 17:10-11).

6. God's Word gives us power to live

a. The Word is full of living power (Hebrews 4:12).

b. The Word protects us from the lies of the devil.
   Matthew 4:4

c. Take time each day to meditate on God's Word.

7. Meditate on God's Word

a. To grow spiritually, we must commune with Jesus.
   John 15:4-5

b. Meditate on the Word day and night (Psalms 1:2-3).

c. Those who live in the Word of God produce spiritual fruit.
   Galatians 5:22-23

Knowing God Through Prayer and Worship

1. Prayer, our communication line with God
  a. Fellowship with the Lord through prayer (Ephesians 6:18).
  b. Prayer may involve speaking in our known language or tongues (1 Corinthians 14:15).

2. Lord, teach us to pray
  a. Jesus lived a life-style of prayer (Luke 5:16; 6:12) setting the example of listening to the voice of the Holy Spirit to direct Him in every situation.
  b. The disciples asked Jesus to teach them to pray (Luke 11:1).

3. A model prayer
  a. Jesus gave His disciples a model prayer (Matthew 6:9-13).
  b. Study this prayer. What have you learned?

4. Let your requests be known
  a. Pray without ceasing (1 Thessalonians 5:17).
  b. Be tenacious in prayer (Luke 11:9-10).
  c. Have an attitude of thanksgiving (Philippians 4:6).

5. Praise and worship brings us to the Father

   a. Worshiping and praising the Lord is included in fellowshipping with God.

   b. Worship focuses on who God is, and praise focuses on what He has done for us.

   c. We must worship from the heart (John 4:23-24).

   d. Offer a sacrifice of praise (Hebrews 13:15).

6. He is worthy to receive praise

   a. Heaven will be a place of worship (Revelation 5:11-12).

   b. A spiritually dead person cannot praise the Lord. Psalms 115:17

   c. God inhabits, or lives in, the praises of His people. Psalms 22:3

7. Expressing worship

   a. Kneel (Psalms 95:6)

   b. Stand and worship (Revelation 7:9-10).

   c. Lift up hands (1 Timothy 2:8).

   d. Be still (Psalms 46:10).

   e. Praise Him with instruments (Psalms 150:3,5).

   f. Dance (Psalms 149:3).

   g. Sing new songs (Psalms 149:1).

   h. Clap and shout (Psalms 47:1).

   i. Speak in psalms, hymns, making melody in your heart. Ephesians 5:19

How Can We Hear God's Voice?

1. **"Is that you, God?"**
   a. It can be a struggle to hear God's voice. When we miss it, we should not hesitate to step out in faith the next time.
   b. Jesus does only what the Father in heaven tells Him. John 8:29

   We, too, can learn to hear clearly from the Father.

2. **Acknowledge God's voice**
   a. Check with the Father about life's decisions and He will lead you (Proverbs 3:5-6).
   b. *Acknowledge* is to *admit the existence, reality or truth of or express gratitude for.*
   c. God may speak to us in dreams, visions, or His audible voice, but He usually speaks by His Word (John 8:31-32) or by His Spirit speaking to our spirits.

3. **God's voice is compatible with God's Word!**
   a. Any dream, prophecy, vision, etc. not lining up with the Word of God is not the voice of God. Scripture is the standard to keep us on track (1 Timothy 3:16-17).
   b. Mature Christians renew their minds on God's Word. Hebrews 5:12-14

4. **Allow the Holy Spirit to enlighten your spirit**
   a. God wants to speak to our spirits by His Spirit. Romans 8:16; Proverbs 20:27
   b. See how the Lord has directed your steps in the past. Proverbs 16:9
   c. God's sheep hear His voice (John 10:4).

5. **Beware of other voices**
   a. Our own voice: We may confuse our desires with the voice of the Lord.
   b. Other people's voices: We may buy into others' philosophies that are hostile to God's Word (2 Corinthians 10:5).
   c. Test it (1 John 4:1).

6. **Enemy talk vs. still small voice**
   a. Another voice we may hear instead of God's: the voice of the enemy who comes as an angel of light.
      2 Corinthians 11:14
   b. Resist the devil. God is greater in you (1 John 4:4).
   c. The voice of God: We most often hear the "still, small voice of God" (1 Kings 19:11-13; Psalms 46:10).

7. **Tuning in to God's voice**
   a. We learn to hear the voice of God through practice and obedience.
   b. Submit to His lordship: silence your own thoughts, desires.
      2 Corinthians 10:5
   c. Resist the enemy: Use the authority Christ has given you to silence the enemy (James 4:7; Ephesians 6:10-20).
   d. Expect an answer: Wait on Him.
      John 10:27; Psalms 69:13; Exodus 33:11

Hearing His Voice Clearly

1. **The struggle to stay on track**
   a. A man loses an ax head (2 Kings 6:1-6). Elisha tells him to go to where he last saw it, and the ax head is found.
   b. If we've lost our way, it is helpful to go back to where we last heard God's voice and remember where our obedience to the Lord declined (Revelation 2:5). Then repent to get back on track.

2. **Go back to where you lost your way**
   a. Jonah disobeyed the Lord but thought back to where he went wrong and repented. God gave him a second chance to obey (Jonah 3:1).
   b. If you have lost your way, the Lord will restore the "lost years" (Joel 2:25). Go back to where you last heard from God.

3. **The Word of God should "align"**
   a. Story of three lighthouses built to warn ships of rocks in harbor. They had to align as the ship sailed into harbor.
   b. To avoid shipwreck in our lives, three "lighthouses" should be aligned: the Word of God, the peace of God, circumstances.
   c. We will not go astray if we obey God's Word. 1 Corinthians 14:37; Joshua 1:8
   d. Satan comes like an angel of light (2 Corinthians 11:14) and tries to deceive us (Galatians 1:6-8). The Word of God is our standard for truth.

4. The peace of God should "align"

a. Having the peace of God is the second "lighthouse" to alert us whether or not we should make a certain decision.

b. How does the peace of God feel to you and how does it affect your life?

5. Circumstances should "align"

a. Timing and circumstances should align before a decision is made.

b. God opened a door for Paul (1 Corinthians 16:8-9). After certain circumstances lined up, Jeremiah knew the message was from God (Jeremiah 32:6-8).

6. God will make it clear

George Mueller gives insights on hearing from God:

a. Get in a state to seek only God's will

b. Combine how the Holy Spirit leads with the Word of God

c. Take into account providential circumstances

d. Through prayer, study of the Word and reflection, you will come to peace about the matter and realize God's will.

7. Listen and communicate!

a. Spend time with God to learn to communicate with Him.

b. Husbands and wives communicate and love each other and grow in relationship together. Jesus wants a similar relationship with us (Ephesians 5:25-27).

Chapter 1
Knowing God Through His Word
Journaling space for reflection questions

*According to John 17:3, how can we get to know God?
Do you know God or only know about Him?*

*Name the three persons of the Trinity. According to Hebrews
11:6, how can we really get to know God?*

*Write down the four reasons confirming that Jesus is who He
said He is. Did Jesus ever deny that He is One with God?*

What does the Word of God do in our lives, according to John 6:63?

How do you know when you mind needs to be renewed? According to Ephesians 5:25-26, what does God use to cleanse us?

How much power does God's Word have?
How do you feed your spirit so that it may grow?

What qualities of Galatians 5:22-23 are produced in your life by meditating on God's Word?

Chapter 2
Knowing God Through Prayer and Worship
Journaling space for reflection questions

Describe prayer in your own words. According to 1 Corinthians 14:15, what two things can a believer pray with?

Why did Jesus withdraw from the world to commune with God? Why did the disciples want to learn to pray as Jesus did?

What have you learned about prayer through studying this model?

What are three possible answers to our prayers? How can we eliminate anxiety from our lives, according to Philippians 4:6?

Explain the difference between praise and worship. What is a true worshiper, according to John 4:23-24?

What happens when we praise God, according to Psalms 149:6-8? How does God live in our praises?

List the physical ways we can express our worship to God. How many do you use when worshiping God?

Chapter 3
How Can We Hear God's Voice?
Journaling space for reflection questions

DAY 1

Why did Jesus have to speak often with His heavenly Father (John 8:29)? Have you ever obeyed what you thought was God's voice and later found it was not? Explain.

DAY 2

What happens when we acknowledge God (Proverbs 3:5-6)? How does God give us truth and how does it set us free (John 8:31-32)?

DAY 3

What is the first step in determining if some thought or word is from God (2 Timothy 3:16-17)? How does God's Word benefit you (Hebrews 5:12-14)?

What are some ways the Lord has spoken to you through he Holy Spirit? Do you always recognize the voice of your Shepherd?

How do we "take captive every thought to make it obedient to Christ"?

Name some ways you resist the devil and his lies. Give examples of times God led you by His still, small voice.

Remember some times when you had to discern between your own voice, the voice of others, the voice of the enemy, and the voice of the Lord. What can you learn from your past that will keep you from making the same mistakes in the future?

Chapter 4
Hearing His Voice Clearly
Journaling space for reflection questions

*Give examples of "ax heads" in your Christian walk.
What does Revelation 2:5 advise us to do?*

*Have you had an experience where you struggled to repent, like
Jonah? What did you do? What should you have done?*

*What are we promised if we obey God's Word (Joshua 1:8)?
What happens if we listen to something other than God's Word
for direction?*

Biblical Foundations

How does the "peace of God" feel and how does it affect your life?

Describe a situation when you had the right direction from the Lord but missed His perfect timing. How did you know?

What does George Mueller mean by "the Spirit and the Word must be combined"?

Describe the relationship Jesus desires to have with His bride— the church. Describe your relationship with Jesus. Ask someone to pray with you to have a more intimate relationship with Jesus.

Daily Devotional Extra Days

If you are using this book as a daily devotional, you will notice there are 28 days in this study. Depending on the month, you may need the three extra days' studies given here.

DAY 29

Come Alive!

Read one verse that "leaped out" at you while you were studying the Word of God in this book. Describe what that verse means to you at this point in your life.

DAY 30

Jesus and You

Read Psalm 139. List ways your relationship with Jesus is growing. Find verses of scripture which describe how Jesus feels about you and how you feel about Him.

DAY 31

Personalize It!

Read Psalm 139 again by inserting your name in wherever it fits. Use this Psalm as a prayer to the Lord.

Biblical Foundations

Coordinates with this series!

Biblical Foundations for Children

Creative learning experiences for ages 4-12, patterned after the *Biblical Foundation Series*, with truths in each lesson. Takes kids on the first steps in their Christian walk by teaching them how to build solid foundations in their young lives. by Jane Nicholas, 176 pages: $17.95 ISBN:1-886973-35-0

Check our Web site: www.dcfi.org

DOVE Christian Fellowship International presents

Hearing God 30 Different Ways Seminar

Learn to "tune in" to God and discern "HIS" voice. God wants to speak to you. Each attendee receives a seminar manual.

Spiritual Fathering & Mothering Seminar

Practical preparation for believers who want to have and become spiritual parents. Each attendee receives a seminar manual.

Elder's and Church Leadership Training

Based on New Testament leadership principles, this seminar equips leaders to provide protection, direction and correction in the local church. Each attendee receives a seminar manual.

Small Groups 101 Seminar

Basics for healthy cell ministry. Session topics cover the essentials for growing cell group ministry. Each attendee receives a *Helping You Build Manual*.

Small Groups 201 Seminar

Takes you beyond the basics and into an advanced strategy for cell ministry. Each attendee receives a seminar manual.

Counseling Basics

This seminar takes you through the basics of counseling, specifically in small group ministry. Includes a comprehensive manual.

Marriage Mentoring Training Seminar

Trains church leaders and mature believers to help prepare engaged couples for a strong marriage foundation by using the mentoring format of *Called Together*. Includes a *Called Together Manual*.

For additional seminars
and more information
www.dcfi.org
Call 800.848.5892
email: info@dcfi.org